ANIMAL BEHAVIOR REVEALED

HOW ANIMALS THINK

REBECCA STEFOFF

Cavendish
Square
New York

This book is dedicated to AUDREY VERONIKA GRAY WILLCOX.

With special thanks to Dr. Michael D. Breed of the environmental, population, and organismic biology department at the University of Colorado, Boulder, for reviewing the text of this book.

Published in 2014 by Cavendish Square Publishing, LLC
303 Park Avenue South, Suite 1247, New York, NY 10010

Library of Congress Cataloging-in-Publication Data
Stefoff, Rebecca
How animals think / Rebecca Stefoff. • p. cm. — (Animal behavior revealed)
Includes bibliographical references and index.
ISBN 978-1-60870-513-9 (hardcover) • ISBN 978-1-62712-024-1 (paperback) • ISBN 978-1-60870-615-0 (ebook)
1. Animal intelligence—Juvenile literature. I. Title.
QL785.S83 2012 • 591.5'13—dc22 • 2010040550

Art Director: Anahid Hamparian • Series Designer: Alicia Mikles

Photo research by Laurie Platt Winfrey, Carousel Research, Inc.

The photographs in this book are used by permission and through the courtesy of:
Cover: Getty Images/ Steve Liss/ Time & Life Pictures; *AGEfotostock:* Louise Murray, 48; *Alamy:* Mary Evans Picture Library, 16; John Cancalosi, 29; Wildlife GmbH, 34; Phil Degginger, 54; Frans Lanting Studio, 61, 64; Zach Holmes, 66; Alamy, 69; *Associated Press;* 39; *Getty Images:* Michael Goldman/ Time & Life Pictures, 4, 58; AFP, 10; Getty Images, 22; Tim Hale, 32; Ben Cranke, 44; *Cavendish Square Publishing, LLC;* 7; *National Geographic Images:* Chris Newbert/ Minden Pictures, 26; *Newscom:* Design Pics, 20; Roger Steene/ AFP/ Getty Images, 35; *Photo Researchers:* Tierbild Okapia, 37; Thomas & Pat Leeson, 41; *Superstock:* Science Faction, 15; *Visuals Unlimited,* Gary Meszaros, 71.

Printed in the United States of America

CONTENTS

INVESTIGATING ANIMAL BEHAVIOR

Imagine that you are talking to someone when suddenly a bird breaks into your conversation—and gives the correct answer to an arithmetic problem. That's what happened to one scientist who was studying the **intelligence** of parrots. An African gray parrot named Alex surprised her by proving that he could add numbers.

Alex's ability to add is just one of the discoveries that are giving scientists new glimpses into animal minds. In recent years researchers have learned that crows create tools, sea lions solve puzzles, and rodents are "mental time travelers" that remember the past. One of the biggest questions in animal research right now is whether animals think. If they do, what do they think about?

People have always been fascinated by animals. Tens of thousands of years ago, our ancestors painted lifelike pictures of bears, bison, and deer on cave walls. Twenty-five centuries ago, Greek thinkers wrote about animals and their habits. Those writings were the beginning of **zoology**, the scientific study of animals.

Alex, an African gray parrot, surprised researchers with his grasp of numbers, colors, and shapes. He answered questions such as "What are the blue things?" or "What are the triangles?" by picking out the correct objects.

In time zoologists wondered why animals do the things they do. When a baby monkey shows fear of snakes, for example, is the fear an **instinct**—a built-in pattern of behavior that is programmed into the monkey's genes? Or has the baby learned to be afraid because its mother and the other monkeys in its troop scream and run when they see a snake? Questions like these led to **ethology**, the branch of zoology that studies animal behavior.

Ethology became established as a science in the twentieth century. One of its pioneers was Konrad Lorenz of Austria, who studied the behavior of geese and ducks. When these birds hatch they usually see their mother right away, and afterward they follow her around. Lorenz wondered what would happen if young birds hatched apart from others of their **species**. He experimented with geese and found that newly hatched birds bonded with the first thing they saw. Young geese that bonded with Lorenz followed him around as if he were their mother. Lorenz called this behavior imprinting.

Lorenz published his findings in 1935. The next year he met Nikolaas Tinbergen, a Dutch zoologist who was also curious about how animals react to signals from their environment. Together, Tinbergen and Lorenz studied seagulls and ducks. They discovered that young birds raised by humans showed no fear of round or square cardboard cutouts, but they instinctively recognized dangerous shapes. When cutouts shaped like hawks and eagles flew over their nests, the birds became afraid, even though they had never seen those **predators** before.

Instinct tells baby geese to follow the first thing they see after they hatch—in this case, their mother.

The work of Lorenz and Tinbergen was a step toward understanding animal instincts. In 1973 the two men and Austrian bee expert Karl von Frisch shared a Nobel Prize, one of the highest scientific honors, for their work in the new science of animal behavior.

Tinbergen came up with four key questions to ask about the things that animals do. Today ethologists and animal behavior researchers still use those questions to guide their investigations. The questions are:

- What causes the animal's behavior? Scientists studying problem-solving in birds, for example, might ask whether a bird is trying to obtain food, avoid a predator, or find a mate.

- Does the behavior change over the animal's lifetime? Do young animals learn more easily than old ones do? Is it true that you can't teach an old dog new tricks?

- How does the animal's behavior compare with the way similar species behave? Do gorillas show the same signs of possible intelligence, such as using tools, as their relatives the chimpanzees?

- Does the behavior help or hurt the animal's chances of surviving and reproducing? Imagine that an octopus figures out how to take a cork out of a bottle. Over the long term, will this skill help or harm the octopus, or will it make no difference?

Tinbergen also warned other scientists against **anthropomorphizing**, which means giving human qualities to animals. When we describe animals in human terms, such as saying, "Oh, that bear is sad," we are anthropomorphizing. For a long time, anthropomorphism was strictly forbidden in ethology. In recent years, though, scientists have learned much about the inner lives of animals—how they think, feel, communicate, and play. Thinking that animals are completely different from people may be as big a mistake as thinking that animals are just like people.

The study of animal behavior takes many forms. Some researchers focus on **psychology**, the study of human and animal minds, or on **evolution**, the history of life on Earth. **Sociobiologists** study animals that live in social groups, such as ants and prairie dogs. Behavioral ecologists look at how animals interact with their environments. Other researchers investigate animal communication and emotion.

This book explores animal intelligence, one of the liveliest subjects in biology today. Experts do not always agree about what goes on in animals' minds, but with each new discovery we come closer to understanding the inner lives of the creatures around us.

1. CLEVER CREATURES

A **skinny finger of land** called Cape Peninsula points out into the sea at the tip of South Africa. Tourists travel to Cape Peninsula to visit the bustling city of Cape Town, to drive through the area's beautiful landscapes, and to encounter animals. If they are lucky, visitors will see wildlife—maybe a colony of beach-dwelling penguins. Unlucky visitors will have their picnics and backpacks stolen by baboons.

Baboon Break-ins

Baboons are monkeys, members of the **primate** family. (Humans are primates, too.) The baboons are at home in the rocky brush of Cape Peninsula, but they now share the area with a large and growing human population. Baboons and people often come into contact, and the baboons have learned that houses and cars may contain tasty treats. For these large, strong monkeys, breaking in to steal human food can be easier than looking for fruit, lizards, and bird eggs in the wild.

Baboons aren't simply smart enough to open cars so they can search inside for food. They're smart enough not to waste their time on cars that they have heard being locked.

Car Doors and Chirping Gadgets

Drivers who stop at scenic spots along the roads of Cape Peninsula might be surprised to see baboons walking along rows of cars, trying to open each car's doors. If a door is unlocked, the baboon will open it and jump inside the car—even if there are people in it. This can be scary and dangerous. A baboon's sharp teeth are as long as a lion's fangs. Baboons aren't really interested in attacking people, though. They just want food, and they have been known to trash the inside of a car, or run off with bags, in search of food.

In 2010 the baboons took their scavenging to a new level. Some of them started walking past certain cars without bothering to test the doors. But why?

The baboons had learned to recognize the chirping sound of the electronic gadgets that drivers use to lock and unlock most new cars. They knew that the sound meant that all doors on that particular car were locked. Baboons watched people pull up and park. If the baboons heard the telltale chirp, they didn't waste their time on that car—they just moved on to one that hadn't chirped.

How Smart Are Baboons?

Baboons are extremely intelligent, says a Cape Town wildlife manager whose job is protecting baboons and humans from each other. By skipping over locked cars, baboons save time and effort, which certainly seems smart. Some scientists, though, would say that the baboons' behavior isn't necessarily a sign of advanced intelligence. It might be the result of **conditioning.**

Conditioning simply means that an animal comes to realize that two things are associated with, or related to, each other. Depending on the species, it may take animals a long time, or not much time at all, to learn that two things are related.

People use conditioning to train their pets. A dog that obeys its owner's commands is rewarded with a treat or with praise and attention, such as a pat on the head and the words "Good dog!" The dog learns to associate the good behavior with the reward. This encourages the dog to repeat the good behavior. But a dog that does something naughty might find itself spending the night in the garage. The owner wants the dog to associate its bad behavior with a result it will not enjoy.

Animal researchers often use conditioning when they are studying how laboratory animals behave. Suppose a scientist wants to see how quickly a rat can learn to go through a square hole instead of a round or triangle-shaped hole. When the rat goes through the square hole, the scientist gives the rat a food treat. If the rat goes through the round or triangle-shaped hole, it doesn't get a treat. Once the rat associates the square hole with food, it chooses the square hole most of the time.

The baboons of Cape Peninsula learned to associate the chirping sound with the result "can't get into the car." Without knowing how long it took the baboons to learn this association, or how many of them have learned it, scientists can't be sure what the behavior says about the baboons' brainpower.

Animal intelligence is an amazing topic, but it is extremely hard to study. Often, scientific research on animal thinking leads not directly to answers but to more questions.

Scientists who study how animals think, or how smart animals are, say a lot of things like "might," "maybe," and "there could be a different explanation." No matter how many tests, experiments, and measurements the experts do, it is hard to know what's going on inside an animal's mind.

The Ghost of Clever Hans

Scientists who work with animals learned an important lesson from a German horse that became a world-famous celebrity in the early years of the twentieth century. The horse was named Clever Hans. Many experts thought that Hans was more than just clever—they thought he was the smartest animal that had ever lived. In 1904 the *New York Times* called Hans "Berlin's Wonderful Horse," and added, "He Can Do Almost Everything but Talk." Although Hans died long ago, his story haunts every modern scientist who is curious about animal intelligence.

A Genius among Horses

Hans belonged to a retired schoolteacher named Wilhelm von Osten, who was curious about whether animals could be taught to understand numbers. Von Osten tried to teach a bear and a cat to add. Unfortunately, neither of these animals showed an interest in arithmetic. Von Osten then bought the horse and taught it to count by tapping a hoof on the ground—once for one, twice for two, and so on.

BRAIN SIZE AND BRAINPOWER

An average human brain weighs about 3 pounds (1.4 kilograms). A squirrel's brain weighs much less—just one-fifth of an ounce (6 grams). That seems to make sense. Humans are more intelligent than squirrels—aren't they?

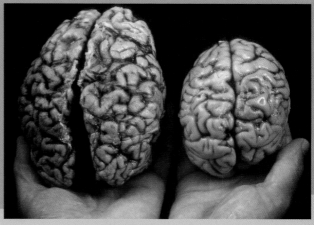

Although a human brain (*left*) is bigger than a gorilla brain, intelligence does not depend on brain size alone.

Squirrels have excellent memories. They can remember hundreds of places where they have hidden nuts or seeds. This mental power is very useful in the food-storing life of a squirrel. Humans, though, clearly have a higher degree of overall intelligence than squirrels. Is that because their brains are bigger?

Humans don't have the biggest brains in the world. A dolphin's brain weighs 3.7 lb. (1.7 kg), and an elephant's brain weighs up to 11 lb. (5 kg). The largest brain ever measured belonged to a sperm whale and weighed 19.6 lb. (8.9 kg). Does that mean that these animals are smarter than humans?

Not necessarily. When it comes to brains, bigger doesn't always mean better. Brain size and brainpower are not the same.

Animals that are big all over have big brains. The creature with the largest brain, the sperm whale, is also one of the largest animals that has ever lived. On the other hand, a squirrel is a lot smaller than a human being, so naturally its brain is smaller, too.

To compare the brain sizes of different species, scientists use mathematical formulas that make up for the differences in overall body weight from species to species. Humans, chimpanzees, and dolphins have the biggest brains relative to their total size.

But size isn't the only important thing about a brain. The brains of some species, including humans, chimps, and dolphins, have more folds, grooves, and bumps on their surfaces than others. Some scientists think that more folding equals a greater ability to process information—in other words, to think.

Das lesende und rechnende Pferd, mit seinem Lehrer HERRN von OSTEN (Berlin.)

Wilhelm von Osten created a letter-and-number board for his "genius" horse, Clever Hans. The horse replied to questions by tapping its hoof a certain number of times for each letter of the answer.

Before long, word got around that von Osten's horse could solve math problems. Hans also answered questions by spelling out words. Von Osten had painted the letters of the alphabet in rows and columns on a board. When Hans was asked a question, such as "What color is this lady's hat?" he spelled out the answer by tapping his hoof. The number of taps stood for the row and column of each letter in the answer.

Crowds flocked to see Hans perform. Some thought that von Osten was a fraud who had trained Hans in the same way circus animals are trained to do tricks. By using food as a reward for good performance, von Osten could have conditioned Hans to recognize a couple of hand signals. He could then use these signals to tell the horse when to start and stop tapping. If this was true, then von Osten was solving the problems while pretending that Hans was doing the thinking.

But there was no sign that von Osten was trying to trick people or to make money from Hans. Instead, von Osten seemed to believe that Hans truly was a genius among horses. At von Osten's suggestion a group of experts, including teachers and scholars, a horse trainer, a magician, a veterinarian, and two zoo directors, examined Hans. The experts agreed that von Osten was not cheating. In fact, Hans answered questions from the experts themselves, and from other people as well.

In the end, the experts announced that Clever Hans was as intelligent as a thirteen- or fourteen-year-old human. Was this really possible?

The Secret of Hans

A student named Oskar Pfungst finally solved the riddle of Clever Hans. Pfungst tested Hans's abilities in all kinds of conditions—in daylight, at dusk, with the horse blindfolded, and with the questioner concealed inside a tent. He discovered that Hans didn't always give the right answer.

Hans answered correctly only under two conditions. First, the horse had to be able to see the person who asked the question. If Hans wore a blindfold, or the question came from someone hidden in a tent, the horse was stumped. Second, the person who asked the question had to know the correct answer. If someone who did not know what the capital of China was asked Hans to spell out the capital of China, the horse could not answer.

The only explanation was that Hans was somehow "getting" the correct answers from the people who asked the questions. After months of tests, however, Pfungst was sure that the many people who asked questions were not cheating.

The questioners weren't cheating, but they *were* giving Hans the answers all along. Pfungst finally realized how the horse performed his wonderful feats. The student noticed that whenever someone asked Hans a question, the questioner tended to lean forward very slightly. Hans would then start tapping. When Hans had tapped his way up to the correct answer, the questioner would relax a little, or maybe give a small lift of the head or a faint sigh. At that point Hans would stop tapping.

The movements made by the people who asked questions were very tiny, and the questioners had no idea that they were making them. Hans could not really add, multiply, or answer questions about the colors of women's headgear. But the horse was clever enough to recognize signals from the people around him, signals so small that the people didn't even know they were sending them.

Getting a Cue

The case of Clever Hans is a good example of why animal intelligence is hard to study. When an animal does something that looks like intelligent or problem-solving behavior, the animal might simply be reacting to signals from the people who are studying it.

Social cueing is the term scientists use for the signals that people and animals pick up from each other all the time. These signals help them "read" each other and get along. A human baby, for example, soon learns a major social cue: the smile, which usually causes people to smile back. For a horse, the sight of other horses peacefully grazing is a social cue that says, "There's food here, and no predators in sight."

Social cues can travel between species. Most humans know that when a dog flattens its ears, shows its teeth, and snarls, it is feeling hostile. The dog's behavior is a cue to stay away from it. Cues travel in the other direction, too. A trained dog understands the cues its human gives to it through words such as "sit" or "here, boy." Many dogs don't even need to hear the commands. Hand gestures work just as well as words.

Horses are also good at picking up cues from people. For thousands of years people have bred horses as domestic animals. Because early breeders favored horses that were peaceful and easy to tame, modern horses tend to be trainable. They have become sensitive to social cues from the humans around them. In addition, horses are good at noticing movements, especially actions that happen on either side of them.

Social cues were the answer to the riddle of Clever Hans. The tiny movements that the horse picked up from the people who asked questions were involuntary social cues. This means that the cues came from people who did not mean to give cues, or know that they were giving them.

The Clever Hans story shows how easy it is for an honest person, like von Osten, to "help" an animal do what the human hopes it will do. Scientists who study animal intelligence must always remember Clever Hans. Just as von Osten's tiny movements cued Hans to tap out his answers, a scientist's tone of voice or body language might cue the behavior of animals being studied.

The best experiments are designed in a way that prevents any social cues from reaching the animals. This is not always possible, and at times scientists work face-to-face with the animals they study. Some of the researchers who have taught sign language to chimpanzees or who have explored the surprising problem-solving skills of African gray parrots have formed close bonds with the animals they've studied. These relationships have led to new ideas about animal intelligence, but some of the ideas are hard to prove or even test. Fortunately, scientists have many ways to investigate animal intelligence.

Domestic horses like these are easy to train, as well as highly alert to human behavior. They pick up many of the same social cues, or signals, that people use when communicating with each other.

2. ANIMALS AND INTELLIGENCE

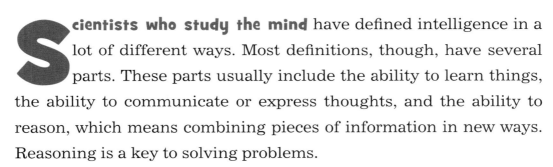

Scientists who study the mind have defined intelligence in a lot of different ways. Most definitions, though, have several parts. These parts usually include the ability to learn things, the ability to communicate or express thoughts, and the ability to reason, which means combining pieces of information in new ways. Reasoning is a key to solving problems.

Intelligence is not just one thing, but a combination of qualities or abilities. And it is hard to measure. Psychologists measure people's intelligence with questionnaires or tools such as the IQ test. (IQ stands for intelligence quotient, and quotient means amount or measure.) Many experts, though, claim that these tools are not always accurate or reliable. There is no perfect way to measure and compare human intelligence. Animal intelligence is an even bigger challenge. Instead of asking, "How intelligent are dogs?" most researchers look at specific kinds of mental activity, such as how many spoken words a dog can

Dogs can learn to perform feats such as smelling for chemicals and rescuing people, but does that equal intelligence? A human-based definition of intelligence does not cover the many kinds of mental activity in the animal world.

learn. This approach has shown that the world of animal **cognition** is rich and full of surprises.

Studying Animals' Mental Lives

If measuring intelligence in people is tricky, measuring it in animals is even harder. For one thing, animals can't answer questions. For another, our notions of intelligence are human-centered—which makes sense, because we're human. We might have some idea what intelligence is to us, but we don't know what it means for animals. Are dogs more intelligent than owls because dogs can be trained to guide blind people and locate earthquake victims? Are foxes more intelligent than dogs because foxes are better at surviving in the wild?

A useful term in animal research is cognition, which is broader and less human-centered than intelligence. Cognition is mental activity or behavior. It covers all kinds of mental processes, both simple and complex. These processes include sensing things, being aware, reacting to events or sense impressions, making decisions, remembering, and reasoning. A key part of cognition, many biologists think, is something called mental time travel. This means that an animal is able to separate itself from the moment in which it is living to remember past experiences or plan future actions.

Instead of trying to invent an overall IQ test for animals, researchers now focus on specific mental activities, such as solving problems, using tools, or counting. They can measure and compare how individual animals perform these activities. In 2010, for example, a psychologist in South Carolina made the news when his dog,

Chaser, was shown to understand the meaning of 1,022 words—more than any other known dog in the world.

Problem Solvers

Animals often astonish people by finding ways to get what they want. Baboons open sealed cars to get at food, for example, and parrots get out of cages that seem escape-proof.

Feats like these impress us, but are they really signs of cleverness? They may simply be the result of luck or trial and error. When a raccoon gets into a food cooler and devours the picnic dinner, for example, did the raccoon figure out how to work the cooler's latch, or did the animal just keep fiddling with the latch until it popped open?

An animal's success at solving a problem may come from luck, patience, or problem-solving skill. Still, some creatures have shown unexpected abilities to figure things out.

Octopuses and Trick Clams

No one expected octopuses to be smart. The Greek scientist and philosopher Aristotle studied animals several thousand years ago. He wrote that the octopus was "a very stupid animal."

The octopus is an **invertebrate**, an animal without a bony spine. That puts the octopus, which doesn't even have a skull, in the same group with clams and snails, and sets it apart from the animals that have spines, which are fishes, amphibians, reptiles, birds, and mammals. Scientists regarded invertebrates as "lower" animals, which

meant animals not likely to have much mental activity—until they took a closer look at the octopus.

Octopuses and their close relatives, squids and cuttlefish, are called **cephalopods**. These animals have larger brains for their body size than any other invertebrates. In fact, cephalopod brains are bigger than fish and amphibian brains as well. Over the years researchers have learned other surprising things about octopuses. For example, these cephalopods can be taught to recognize shapes. They have good memories, and they can use their sucker-covered tentacles like hands, to move and twist things.

Biologists who keep octopuses in aquariums do a lot of things to challenge the animals. A keeper might place an octopus's favorite foods, such as clams, inside a see-through bottle or box. Most of the time, the octopus will quickly figure out how to unscrew the bottle top or open the box.

Two scientists designed an experiment to test octopuses' problem-solving skills. They gave the animals a type of clam that is usually easy for octopuses to eat. The octopuses simply pull the clamshells open with their strong tentacles to get at the soft meat inside. This time, though, the experimenters wired the clams shut.

When the octopuses discovered that they couldn't pull the clams open, they stopped trying. Instead, they used their sharp, tongue-like organs, called radulas, to drill through the clamshells. Octopuses generally drill only when dealing with other kinds of clams that can't be pulled open. In this experiment, the octopuses first tried to open

Octopuses have been called "the smartest animals without skeletons." Prying open a giant clam is instinctive, but people who work with octopuses know that these eight-armed creatures are also good at solving problems.

the "easy" clams using the easy method. When that didn't work, they quickly shifted gears and used the "hard" clam method to open the easy clams. This result showed that octopuses change their behavior to fit unusual conditions, such as getting into clams that should be easy to open, but aren't.

Keas and Locked Boxes

Keas are green parrots that live in the mountains of New Zealand, in the southern Pacific Ocean. They are active, curious birds, always interested in new and unfamiliar things. They seem to enjoy using their claws and sturdy beaks to manipulate, or handle and move, objects. However, the kea's curiosity and playfulness can be destructive. People who live in kea country tell of windshield wipers and radio antennas pulled off cars by the birds.

To find out how keas solve problems, researchers test the birds' ability to manipulate things to get something they want. The experimenters place a piece of fruit—a favorite food of keas—inside a clear plastic box. The lid of the box can be fastened shut with various arrangements of bolts, screws, locks, and rods. To get the fruit, a kea must unlock one or more of these fasteners, and then open the lid of the box.

Can a kea learn how to solve a problem, such as opening a box lock, by watching another bird? To find out, researchers fastened the box with a pin, a plastic screw, and a bolt all at the same time. Then they trained one group of keas to open the box by manipulating the three fasteners. Afterward, another group of keas, the observers, were

With a strong beak and claws, a kea can strip a car of its windshield wipers in minutes. Because these parrots seem to enjoy twisting and pulling objects, scientists test them with puzzle boxes that the keas must unlock and open to get at the fruit inside.

allowed to watch the trained birds open the box. The third group of keas was the control group. The control birds received no training and did not observe the trained birds opening the box.

Each bird in the observer and control groups got three chances to open the box. The experimenters discovered that the two groups took different approaches to the problem. Control birds spent time pecking and nibbling at the box itself. Observer birds, which had seen a trained kea at work, went straight to the fasteners. Two observers managed to open all three fasteners, and every observer opened at least one fastener.

The control birds didn't do so well. Some of them didn't open any of the fasteners. Others opened only one fastener. No control kea opened all three fasteners.

The experiment showed that keas use social learning—that is, they can learn new things by watching other keas. The observer keas did not seem to learn anything as detailed as "first pull this pin, then turn this screw, then push this bolt." Instead, researchers think, the observers picked up a more general kind of information, something like "if you fiddle around with these gadgets on top of the box, you can open the box."

Most of the keas that opened the fasteners succeeded through trial and error, not by following an exact series of steps. Still, watching the trained keas definitely gave the observers a head start over the control group. The observers went to work on the fasteners more quickly than the controls did, and they did not give up as easily.

Could keas improve their box-opening performance by just examining the box, without watching trained birds open it? In 2010 researchers at Kyoto University in Japan reported on an experiment designed to answer that question. They also tested keas with plastic boxes and multiple fasteners. Some keas got to study the box for a while before trying to open it. Most of the time, the keas that had this "preview" of the box didn't open it faster than birds that hadn't had a chance to see or study the box first. But in the hardest stage of the experiment, the birds had to open one bolt in order to reach a second bolt beneath it. When the keas tried to solve this complex problem, the birds that had previewed the box opened it faster than the rest of the birds did.

WHERE'S THE TOY?

Anyone with a pet dog or cat can do an easy experiment to test the workings of the animal's mind. The equipment is simple: you'll need a toy that the animal likes, an empty can or other container big enough to hold the toy, and three boxes with sides tall enough to hide the container. (A few food treats for the pet might come in handy, too.) Two people are needed to do the experiment.

Set the three boxes in a row on the floor. Show the pet the toy, and then toss it across the room. Reward the animal with praise or a treat for going to the toy. Next, have one person hold the pet so that it can see the boxes. Then have the other person put the toy into one of the boxes, letting the animal watch.

Now let the dog or cat search for the toy. If the pet goes first to the box with the toy, the experiment is a hit, or success. If the pet goes first to a different box, it's a miss, or failure. Repeat until the animal gets bored, using a different box each time.

This experiment tests a mental tool called **object permanence.** Object permanence is the ability to know that objects still exist even when they can't be seen. After watching the toy disappear into a box, the animal knows the toy is there inside the box.

Human babies develop object permanence around eight months of age. Many animals have object permanence, too. Among them are chickens, hamsters, monkeys, apes, cats, and dogs. (Not every cat or dog passes the test, though. To find out whether a species has object permanence, scientists have to test a lot of animals in that species.)

For a more challenging test, let the cat or dog watch as one experimenter places the toy *inside* the can or container. Next, put the container behind one of the boxes, then turn the container over, making sure that the animal can't see or hear the toy come out of the container. Now take the container from behind the box and show the animal that it is empty. Where does the animal look for the toy? The experiment is a success if the animal goes first to the box with the toy behind it.

This second test is called the invisible displacement test. To pass it, an animal has to understand that the toy can be inside the container. Then, when the animal sees the empty container, it must realize that the toy came out of the container while the container was hidden behind the box. Finally, the animal has to remember which box was used. This series of mental steps seems rare in the animal world. Only humans, chimpanzees, gorillas, and adult dogs have passed the invisible displacement test. Some researchers claim that parrots, monkeys, and cats have passed it, too, but there's not enough evidence to be sure.

A dog's favorite toy can be used in a simple test to see if the animal has a mental ability called object permanence.

The Japanese researchers decided that the keas mostly used "explorative strategies," which is a scientific term for trial and error, or trying a lot of different approaches until one works. But in the most complex test, keas performed better with advance information. The scientists don't yet know whether the successful birds planned the right moves ahead of time, or were better at recognizing and correcting the wrong moves.

Tool Users and Toolmakers

For a long time people believed that only humans used tools. Then, in 1960, an ape researcher named Jane Goodall saw wild chimpanzees sticking twigs into termite mounds, then pulling out the twigs with termites on them. The chimps were using the twigs to "fish" for termites to eat. This discovery launched a search for other examples of animals using tools, both in the wild and in captivity. Scientists now know dozens of species that are tool users, and the list gets longer all the time.

Invertebrates: Spineless Tool Users?

Even though they do not have backbones, octopuses might still be tool users. It all depends on how "tool use" is defined.

Because octopuses don't have bones, they are very flexible. They can squish and twist their bodies into tiny places. They like to hide out in small holes or crannies in rocks and reefs, or even in thrown-away bottles and cans on the ocean floor. They sometimes reach out of their hidey-holes, pick up nearby rocks with their tentacles, and pile

them outside the holes. The octopuses appear to be building walls for protection while they sleep.

Octopuses have been filmed carrying empty coconut shells across bare, sandy stretches of sea bottom. If something startles the octopus, it drops the shell and scoots inside it, turning the shell into an instant hiding place.

Are the rocks and coconut shells tools? Some

An octopus carries a coconut shell to use as an emergency shelter on bare ocean floor. Is the shell a tool? Scientists do not agree on the answer.

scientists say no. They say that the octopuses are just following their instincts to seek shelter, in the same way that birds build nests or hermit crabs move into the abandoned shells of other sea creatures. In these scientists' view, an animal isn't using a tool unless it manipulates an object to change the environment.

Stacking the rocks might count as tool use because it does change the octopus's environment. However, the majority of scientists say that although a rock wall might protect an octopus from possible danger in the future, true tool use means solving a problem in the present. By that definition, octopuses are not yet known to use tools.

A stick for fishing termites out of a hole was the first tool that scientists saw chimpanzees using. Other animals also make and use tools, which used to be considered human-only behavior.

Birds: Is a Car a Tool?

Seagulls drop oysters on rocks to crack open their shells. Crows and blue jays drop nuts on streets and parking lots to crack the nutshells open on the pavement. Are these birds using the rocks and pavement as tools? What if a crow dropped a nut where a car would run over it and open it? Would the car be the crow's tool?

Animal researchers don't agree. Good scientific studies of wild birds opening food by dropping it are rare. It's not yet proven, for example, that birds deliberately use moving cars to crack nutshells. And not all scientists would agree that pavements and cars are tools, because the birds don't manipulate them. But everyone agrees that when an Egyptian vulture picks up a rock in its beak and then drops the rock to break open an ostrich egg, the vulture is using a tool.

Burrowing owls may be tool users, too. These birds, which live in holes in the ground in the western United States, use other animals' feces as bait. The owls collect dung from mammals such as cattle and scatter it around their burrows. The dung attracts beetles, which then are eaten by the owls.

Woodpecker finches are birds that live in the Galapagos Islands. They eat insects and grubs that they find on leaves, in moss, or in the bark of trees. These finches obtain about half of their food by using tools to probe into places where their beaks won't fit. The finches pick up twigs or cactus spines with their beaks, then jab these tools into thick moss or leaves or into small holes or cracks in tree bark. The finches use the tools to poke beetles and other **prey** out into the open, where they can be eaten.

Chimpanzees are not the only animals that fish. This woodpecker finch in the Galapagos Islands uses a cactus spine to jab insects and larva and pull them out of holes.

Birds: Crafty Crows

The superstar tool users of the bird world are New Caledonian crows. These birds are native to a few islands in the South Pacific. In the 1990s, after people reported seeing wild crows use tools, researchers went to New Caledonia to investigate. Some of their early studies involved capturing wild birds and attaching tiny "crow-cams" to them to record their activities. Other scientists took a different approach. They raised some of the crows in captivity and then designed experiments to test the birds' tool-using abilities.

New Caledonian crows start making and using tools when they are about ten weeks old, even if they have never seen other crows or people using tools. Like Egyptian vultures and woodpecker finches, the crows use tools to get food. But the crows don't just pick up a rock or a cactus spine that happens to be lying around. They *make* tools, selecting different materials for different purposes and then shaping those materials.

One type of tool is made from the edge of the stiff, barbed leaves of the pandanus plant. The crow cuts a strip of leaf with its beak and then nips it into a long, pointed shape. New Caledonian crows are also the first animals known to make and use hooks. The birds select a twig with a smaller twig branching from it and then break off the smaller twig so that its stub forms a hook. With this tool the crow can pull and pry at pieces of bark that it could not move with a straight stick. Other materials for toolmaking include vines, feathers, and leaf stems. Crows have been seen carrying tools in their beaks from one feeding site to another, and tucking the tools under their feet while eating.

Captive crows make tools out of materials not available to wild crows, such as lengths of wire. A female crow named Betty even invented her own way to make a hook out of flexible wire. She pushed one end of a piece of wire into a small hole in the wall of her room until the wire bent, forming a hook. Betty stuck the wire hook into a deep plastic tube to snag a small pail of food—something she couldn't reach any other way.

Betty also solved a puzzle called the stick-and-tube puzzle. She was given two objects: a stick and a clear plastic tube. The tube was

Caledonian crows are champion toolmakers. A tiny video camera mounted among this bird's tail feathers may let researchers watch as it shapes twigs into hooks.

fastened into a wooden frame so that she couldn't shake or handle it. In the middle of the tube was a piece of food. The only way Betty could get the food was to poke the stick into one end of the tube and use it to push the food out the other end. Before Betty, only primates—apes and one species of monkey—had ever solved the stick-and-tube puzzle. Betty solved it, and so have other New Caledonian crows.

These remarkable birds can even solve complex problems that require the use of multiple tools. In 2007, scientists in New Zealand reported a breakthrough in the study of captive New Caledonian crows. Birds had been shown two boxes. One box contained food. The other contained a long stick. The crows could not reach either box. The birds were then given a stick. The stick was too short to reach the food box, but it was long enough to reach the box that contained the longer stick. To get the food, the crows would have to use the shorter stick to reach the box with the longer stick, and then use the longer stick to reach the box with the food.

Six out of seven crows solved the problem correctly on their first try, something that only apes had done before. To do this, they had to follow a series of mental steps. First, they had to see the difference in length between the two sticks. Next, they had to decide not to try for the food box first. They had to understand that if they worked on getting the long stick instead, they would eventually get the food. To reach their ultimate goal, the birds used one tool to get hold of another tool, showing a clear example of reasoning by animals outside the primate family.

Marine Mammals: With and Without Hands

Sea otters are well known for their use of tools. These mammals live in the ocean, and their primary food is the meat of clams and other shelled creatures. When an otter can't crack a shell with its sharp teeth, it picks up a rock from the seafloor. Floating on its back with the rock resting on its chest or stomach, the otter grips the clam with both front paws and pounds it against the rock to break the shell.

Rocks also come in handy as undersea hammers. If a snail clings so tightly to the stony seafloor that an otter can't pull it loose, the

A sea otter feasts on the meat of a clam. It opened the clam by pounding it against the rock balanced on its stomach.

otter pounds the prey free with a rock. When an otter finds a rock tool of a useful size and shape, it may carry the rock around in its "pocket"—a pouch of loose skin on its chest.

Otters are good at manipulating things with their paws, but wild bottlenose dolphins that live in Shark Bay, Australia, manage to use tools even though they don't have paws or hands.

These sea mammals have a narrow beak called a rostrum on the front of their head. When scientists saw a Shark Bay bottlenose dolphin with a lump on her rostrum, they thought it was a tumor. A closer look showed that it was a sea sponge. Dolphins often poke the seafloor with their rostrums to stir up small fish, shrimp, and other prey, so the scientists thought that one dolphin had poked its rostrum into a sponge that had become stuck on the animal.

Then the scientists started seeing sponges on the rostrums of a few other dolphins. A sudden flurry of accidental sponge attachments did not seem likely. What was going on?

Divers took cameras underwater to investigate. They discovered that dolphins were examining patches of sea sponges and selecting sponges of the right size and shape to fit like nose guards over their rostrums. With the sponges in place, the dolphins probed the seabed. Scientists now think that the dolphins use the sponges to protect their rostrums from being cut by coral or stung by poisonous bottom-dwelling stonefish.

During the 1990s divers recorded the dolphins' use of sponges. But only a few of the dolphins around Shark Bay were spongers, and no one had seen dolphins sponging anywhere else. All but one of the sponging dolphins were female. Why did some dolphins sponge, while most did not? To find out whether the behavior had something to do with relationships among the Shark Bay dolphins, researchers tested the DNA of 13 spongers and 172 non-spongers, looking for a pattern.

In 2005 the researchers reported their findings. Nearly all of the spongers were closely related, descended from the same female ancestor. The best explanation for this pattern is that one female dolphin started sponging—no one knows why or how—and then taught her daughters to do it, or they copied her. The next generation of females learned to sponge from their mothers, and so on.

Scientists can't yet explain why male dolphins almost never sponge. Research to investigate this and other questions about tool-using dolphins is taking place beneath the surface of Shark Bay right now.

Primates: Monkeys, Orangutans, and Gorillas

Ever since Jane Goodall discovered in 1960 that chimpanzees use tools, scientists have paid a lot of attention to tool use by non-human primates. Some monkeys use tools, and so do the great apes: orangutans, gorillas, and chimpanzees.

Capuchins, also called white-faced monkeys, are small monkeys native to Central and South America. In the wild they use several kinds of tools. With sticks or twigs they pry insects out of tree bark and logs. They break open rotten logs or stumps by pounding them with small branches to get at the insects and grubs inside. They also place hard-shelled palm nuts on rocky ground and then drop heavy

stones on them to crack the shells. Some capuchins do this in the same spot so often that they create a permanent hollow or bowl in the rocky ground.

Experiments with tame and captive capuchins show that these monkeys shape their tools. They break or split sticks into the desired shape. Some capuchins use stones to hammer bones into a new size and shape, and then use the bones as tools. This makes researchers think that capuchins are able to form a plan or mental picture of the tool they want to create.

Orangutans live on Sumatra and Borneo, two islands in Southeast Asia. Their normal habitat is dense forest. The first orangutans that were seen using tools were captive or semi-captive animals in zoos or wildlife refuges. Then, in 1994, a primate researcher saw wild orangutans using tools. In a swampy region of Sumatra, orangutans were using sticks to break into a fruit called the puwin, which is covered with needlelike spines. The orangutans of Borneo, however, have not yet been seen using tools.

Why do orangutans use tools on one island but not the other? Scientists think tool use spread throughout the Sumatran population because those orangutans live close together in the flooded forest and are more social. Therefore, the primates probably saw one or two individuals using sticks to get at the nutritious fruit and copied that behavior. On Borneo, individual orangutans live alone and spend little time around other orangutans. They wouldn't have the chance to see other primates using tools.

Palm nuts, like clams, are hard to open. A capuchin monkey solves the problem with a large rock.

The gorillas of Central Africa are the largest great apes. Until 2005, **primatologists** thought that gorillas did not use tools. Then a group of researchers who had been studying a band of the animals for ten years became the first to see wild gorillas using tools. A female gorilla broke a branch from a tree and used it as a walking stick when she walked into a water hole. Gorillas are not good swimmers, and the stick may have helped the animal do two things: keep her balance and judge how deep the water was before each step. The same group of researchers photographed another gorilla, also female, as she moved a tree stump to use as a seat, and then poked the ground with a stick, digging for plants to eat.

Chimpanzees: Our Closest Relatives

Among the chimpanzees of Africa, our closest primate relatives, females make a bigger variety of tools, and use them more often, than do the males. They pass the knowledge and skills of tool use on to young chimpanzees, which learn by watching and copying their mothers.

Wild chimpanzees across Africa use at least thirty-five different kinds of tools. They crack palm nuts open between two flat stones. To get water from holes in trees, they chew leaves and ball them up into "sponges" that will absorb the water.

One common chimpanzee tool is a heavy stick used as a club to smash beehives or cola nuts. In a few cases chimpanzees have been seen using clubs to hit other chimps, or to strike at prey, such as birds. (Chimpanzees are known to make organized war on other chimps. Bands of male chimps attack members of rival bands, sometimes wielding sticks as weapons. In 2010 researchers who had observed a ten-year-long chimpanzee war reported that the conflict was probably over territory.)

Chimpanzees, like many other animals, use tools to probe for food. Jane Goodall's original sighting of the termite fishing stick is a good example of what scientists call extractive tool use. In this type of tool use, an animal uses a tool to extract, or pull out, food that it can't reach.

Pulling bugs out of a termite nest with a stick is not the same thing as making a weapon for the purpose of hunting for prey. Before 2007, scientists thought that only humans did that. Then scientists in southern Senegal reported something new. Female chimpanzees were making sticks into spears, sharpening the ends with their teeth, and using these weapons to reach into tree nests to stab sleeping bush babies, small animals in a different branch of the primate family. The hunters then ate the bush babies or fed them to their offspring. This is the first known case of animals making weapons to use for hunting other animals.

So far, only one group of Senegalese chimpanzees is known to make spears. This is no surprise to primatologists, because not all chimps use the same tools. Various chimp populations have their own tool kits, or sets of tools used by the chimps in each region. Animal researchers see this as a sign that chimpanzees possess cultures, which are bodies of knowledge that are learned and taught, passed from one generation to the next. Human beings have created many cultures that are similar in some ways and different in others. The same thing seems to be true of chimpanzees.

3. USING SYMBOLS, NUMBERS, AND WORDS

Half a century ago, people thought only humans had tools and language. We now know of many animals that use tools. But what about language? Do animals have that, too?

Animals communicate with each other in an amazing variety of ways. Scientists have learned that animal communication is common and often complex. But communication and language are not the same. An animal communicates when it sends or gives off a message that another animal can understand. The message can take many forms, such as a firefly's blinking light, a chemical signal that says that a fish is ready to find a mate, or the thirty-minute song of a humpback whale. In animal communication, each signal or message has a definite meaning.

Language is different. It is more complex and more flexible than communication. Language is a system of rules for combining words in an unlimited number of ways to express an unlimited range of

Nelson, a California sea lion, is part of the U.S. Navy's Marine Mammal Program, which trains the animals to search harbors for swimmers and explosives. Sea lions learn easily, which makes them good subjects for the study of animal intelligence.

meanings. Animal language research is aimed at discovering whether animals have this kind of language, or can learn to use human language.

Animal language research is a fascinating topic. It has introduced the world to a parrot that could add and apes that used sign language. Scientists, though, do not always agree on the meaning of these studies. The question of whether animals can truly communicate with humans in our own languages is still being explored.

It's Symbolic

Human language calls for certain kinds of mental activities. Language users have to grasp abstract ideas, and they must be able to use symbols.

Abstract ideas are not just hard-to-define notions such as justice or beauty. They are ideas that apply to many different situations. For example, "some," "more," "less," "before," and "after" are all abstract qualities. Symbols are things that represent, or stand for, other things. Words act as symbols. The word "apple" symbolizes a particular kind of fruit.

Some animals appear to understand abstract ideas and symbols. Scientists do not yet know how common these abilities are in the animal world, or what they tell us about how animals' minds work.

Sea Mammals and Hand Gestures

Sea lions appear to understand symbols. These large ocean mammals live along coastlines of the Pacific and southern Atlantic Oceans.

They are good subjects for research in animal cognition because they can easily be trained to take part in experiments. In one series of experiments, trainers used conditioning to teach a pair of sea lions to recognize hand gestures. The animals learned that certain gestures referred to either items in their pool or things they could do.

In 1992 the researchers reported that the sea lions could follow complex commands. When a trainer made a series of three gestures, the sea lions understood the relationships among these symbols. If a trainer made the signs for "white ball," "flipper," and "touch," a sea lion would swim to a white ball and touch it with its flipper. The animals were processing information that was put together like words in a sentence.

A few years earlier, other scientists had done a similar set of experiments with dolphins in Hawaii. Akeakamai, a dolphin trained to recognize fifty hand gestures, correctly followed commands about 85 percent of the time.

The most interesting thing about the Akeakamai experiments is that the dolphin understood the difference between the commands "pipe hoop fetch" (take the hoop to the pipe) and "hoop pipe fetch" (take the pipe to the hoop). In human terms, Akeakamai had a grasp of **syntax**, which is the way words fit together to give meaning to sentences. The phrases "dog bites man" and "man bites dog" show the importance of syntax. Both phrases have the same three words (like the three gestures in Akeakamai's commands), but a simple switch in word order creates a dramatic change in meaning. Syntax is a vital ingredient of language—one that some animals seem to understand.

A Sea Lion Picks a Picture

A female sea lion called Rio showed a kind of cognition that psychologists call **equivalence**. This means seeing a new relationship between things based on something that the animal already knows. Here's how it worked for Rio:

First, trainers conditioned Rio and another female sea lion named Rocky to match pairs of pictures. The pictures were of random objects such as teapots, keys, and numbers. The researchers showed picture A to one of the sea lions. If she picked picture B to pair with it, she received a fish as a reward. Soon Rio and Rocky learned that when the trainers showed picture A, they should pick picture B. Then when the trainers showed her picture B, she was meant to pick picture C to make a pair with it, and she learned that, too.

Second, the trainers showed picture A to Rio and Rocky but in a new way. This time, to make a pair with picture A, the sea lion could not choose picture B, because the trainers didn't include it. Instead, the animal had to match picture A with either picture C or the newly added picture D. The correct answer was picture C, because the sea lions had already learned that picture A was connected to picture B and picture B was connected to picture C. In other words, picture C had equivalence to picture A. The two pictures were linked by their relationship to picture B, even though picture B was not part of the new experiment. But picture D did not have equivalence. It wasn't in any of the pairs that the sea lions had learned to connect.

Rio picked picture C to pair with picture A, not just once, but many times, even using different sets of images. The scientists who studied the two sea lions felt that Rio had showed logical thinking. She understood that two things (picture A and picture C) that were related to a third thing (picture B) were also related to each other. Rocky had done well at matching the pairs of pictures in the first part of the experiment. When it came to the equivalence test, however, Rocky did not perform as well as Rio. Her results did not show logical thinking the way Rio's did.

Count On It

Experts were embarrassed in 1907 when they were proved wrong about the counting abilities of the horse Clever Hans. For many years afterward, only a few scientists were willing to investigate the question of whether animals can count. Today, though, scientists are once again interested in this subject. They are finding that a lot of species have some kind of number sense.

Number Awareness in Many Species

Laboratory experiments have shown that pigeons, rats, and monkeys understand the concepts of less and more. So do red-backed salamanders. Researchers experimented to see whether these small, forest-dwelling amphibians would choose a clear plastic tube with two flies in it or a clear tube with three flies. All of the salamanders picked the tube with three flies. Scientists think it is likely that many species can tell the difference between smaller and larger quantities.

Crows, ravens, rats, pigeons, and raccoons take number sense a step further. They can learn to recognize specific numbers. For

example, researchers conditioned a raccoon to recognize the number three. The raccoon was shown clear plastic boxes with different numbers of grapes inside, from one to five. Only if it picked the box with three grapes would the raccoon be allowed to open the box and eat the grapes. Raccoons love grapes. Any raccoon would rather have four or five grapes than three, but the raccoons in the experiment learned to recognize the box with three grapes and to choose it every time, because they knew they could open it.

Primate Math

Monkeys and chimpanzees have shown several kinds of numerical ability. Macaque monkeys can be trained to perform well on tests where they must identify quantities as high as four. A chimpanzee named Sheba learned to recognize the number symbols 1, 2, 3, and 4. She could correctly match the symbols to groups of objects, for example, picking a card with "3" on it to go with a tray of three gumdrops.

In another experiment, if Sheba found one orange in one part of her room and two oranges in a different part of the room, she chose the "3" card. With different combinations of oranges totaling zero to four, Sheba was right 80 percent of the time.

Then the experiment changed. Instead of oranges, Sheba found cards with Arabic numerals on them. This time she could not reach the correct answer just by counting the objects she found. For example, if Sheba found two cards, and each card said "2," the correct answer would not be "2" but "4." Again, Sheba picked the correct answer card about 80 percent of the time.

Red-backed salamanders can tell the difference between two flies and three. Many species may have some understanding of qualities such as "less" and "more," even if they cannot count.

Sheba's performance in the card experiment astonished the primatologists who were studying her. Either Sheba had memorized all of the possible combinations and was giving the right answers by memory, or she was doing basic arithmetic and adding. Even though she made mistakes and gave the wrong answer 20 percent of the time, she gave the right answer so often that it could not be due to chance. Researchers are working with chimpanzees and other primates to understand what their number skills truly are.

Teaching Animals to Talk

Dogs and many other species of animals can be trained to obey commands given in words or gestures. This does not mean that the animals understand the meanings of words in the same way that people do. When a dog hears the phrase, "Sit down," and then sits down, the dog has learned through conditioning that sitting down is what people want it to do when it hears those sounds. There's no reason to think that the dog knows that "sitting" is what its human family does on the couch, or that "down" can be used to talk about the basement, the stock market, or somebody's bad mood.

To learn more about how animal minds work, researchers have tried to teach animals to use human language. The most remarkable results have come from experiments with parrots and apes.

A Bird of Many Words

Alex, Irene Pepperberg's African gray parrot, spoke with words as well as numbers. At the time of his death Alex had a vocabulary of about

150 words. This isn't completely unusual for a parrot. These birds have long been famous for copying and repeating things that they hear people say. They also imitate familiar sounds, such as a car horn or the beeping of a microwave oven. Alex was different. He appeared to understand the *meaning* of some of the words in his vocabulary.

At times Alex was most likely simply repeating things he had heard, without truly understanding them. For example, after a researcher started saying "You be good. I love you" to Alex at the end of each day, the bird began repeating the phrase. Alex exchanged those words with Pepperberg or the other researchers when they left him at the end of each day. Alex could have been using the words simply to mean "Goodbye" or "This is what we say at this time," instead of knowing their full meaning.

Clearly, though, Alex did grasp the meaning of many words. He learned to identify colors, shapes, and different kinds of material, such as paper, chalk, and wood. Alex understood that objects could fit into more than one category at the same time. A researcher might show Alex a set of objects including a square piece of green wood, a piece of green chalk, a square piece of blue paper, and a square piece of red wood, and then ask, "What shape is the green wood?" Most of the time Alex would answer "Square." Alex also understood the concepts of bigger, smaller, more, and none.

The secret to Alex's success might be the training method that Pepperberg invented for him. Parrots are social birds that pay a lot of attention to what other birds—or people—are doing. Pepperberg thought that Alex might learn best by seeing someone else do what

ALEX ADDS UP

Irene Pepperberg, a researcher in animal behavior, bought an African gray parrot named Alex from a pet store in Chicago in 1977. She worked with Alex at various universities for thirty years, until he died in 2007. Pepperberg's research with Alex broadened our ideas about the mental abilities of birds.

Alex had a good grasp of numbers up to six. When he was shown a collection of objects and asked "How many?" he spoke the correct answer about 85 percent of the time. In her 2008 book *Alex & Me* Pepperberg tells how she discovered that Alex could add.

Together Alex the parrot and Irene Pepperberg, a psychologist and animal behavior researcher, stretched the boundaries of what scientists knew about birds' abilities.

It happened in 2004, when Pepperberg was teaching another parrot, Griffin, to recognize the number two. She used a computer to produce clicking sounds for Griffin to count. Alex, who already knew his numbers, was in the room, too, in a separate cage from Griffin.

Pepperberg gave two clicks and asked Griffin, "How many?"

She wanted Griffin to say "Two," but he didn't answer.

Pepperberg gave another two clicks and asked Griffin, "How many?"

No answer from Griffin, but this time Alex said, "Four."

"Pipe down, Alex," Pepperberg said. "I'm asking Griffin." She was annoyed. Not only was Alex butting in, but he had given the wrong answer.

Pepperberg tried again with another two clicks. Griffin didn't answer, but Alex did. He said, "Six."

Suddenly Pepperberg realized that Alex might have added up the three sets of two clicks each, for a total of six clicks.

Pepperberg decided to test Alex's ability to add by hiding nuts under cups. She would show him two nuts under one cup, then cover them up and show him three nuts under a different cup, and ask, "How many total nuts?" Pepperberg and other experimenters tested Alex this way over a six-month period. He was right more than 85 percent of the time. Although Pepperberg has not yet gotten similar results with other parrots, Alex showed that at least one African gray parrot could add as well as a small child.

she wanted him to do. She used a student or assistant to act out Alex's role.

Pepperberg would ask a question to Alex and the student at the same time. If Alex did not answer, the student gave the desired answer —and got a reward. Sometimes the student gave the wrong answer on purpose, so that Alex could see Pepperberg shake her head and say "No." The human student not only showed the parrot how the training process was supposed to work but also served as the parrot's rival. Alex's natural love of attention led him to compete with the student for Pepperberg's attention by answering her questions.

Apes and Language

Since the 1960s scientists have been working with apes in a number of long-term language projects. Some researchers teach American Sign Language (ASL) to the animals. Others use a set of symbols, called lexigrams, that represent words. The lexigrams may be magnets that can be stuck to a board, or symbols on a specially designed computer keyboard or touch screen.

Many primates that have performed especially well in language experiments are well known to the public through magazine and newspaper articles, books, and video documentaries. Washoe and Nim were the first chimpanzees to learn more than a hundred ASL signs. Chantek is one of several orangutans that have learned to answer questions in ASL.

A gorilla named Koko, however, may be the primate with the largest ASL vocabulary. Francine Patterson, Koko's trainer, claims that

Koko the gorilla began using sign language to communicate with her trainer, psychologist Francine Patterson. Koko started learning to sign in 1972.

the animal has been documented using more than a thousand signs.

The gorilla has also created new signs, such as combining those for "finger" and "bracelet" to make a sign for "ring." Koko became famous for using ASL to communicate with another gorilla that was her companion, and also for her love of kittens and cats.

Ai is a chimpanzee that has worked with animal language researchers in Japan since 1977. She learned to use lexigrams to identify objects, colors, and numbers. Ai knew the correct lexigrams for "pencil," "blue," and "three," for example. When experimenters showed Ai a new set of objects, she could correctly identify the set as "pencil blue three." Even though Ai was not taught to give the lexigrams in any particular order, she created a structure of her own that she always follows: name, color, number.

Another lexigram-using primate is Kanzi, a bonobo (a species closely related to chimpanzees) raised in captivity. For two years researchers tried to teach Kanzi's mother to use a lexigram keyboard, but she was not a good subject for the experiment. She seemed to have no interest. But young Kanzi had observed his mother's training. He turned out to be very interested. Without any direct training he mastered the use of the keyboard and used it to ask for things he wanted, such as food and toys. Kanzi can now identify about four hundred spoken words by pointing to objects, photographs, or lexigrams that match the words. His trainers report that he understands spoken language at about the level of a two-and-a-half-year-old child.

The Language Puzzle

From the start, animal language studies have stirred up debate in the scientific world. The general public loves to hear about the latest evidence of parrots answering questions or gorillas inventing new words. But while these exciting developments make news, the rest of the story—the animals' mistakes or the long strings of meaningless signs—doesn't usually get reported.

Breakthroughs in animal communication can look a bit different when they are seen as pieces of a bigger picture. A good example comes from 1977, when a chimp named Lana was shown an orange and described it with a string of three lexigrams: "apple," "which-is," "orange-color." Lana had combined three symbols she already knew to create a name for a new object that was a fruit, like an apple, but was orange in color rather than red. Exciting news!

But the complete exchange between Lana and Tim, the trainer, is less exciting. Tim shows Lana the orange and asks her what color it is. She answers that it is orange, and then asks for a red cup. Next Lana names another trainer who is not in the room. Then Lana gives the symbol for "eye" before asking Tim to give her the orange item:

"Tim give which-is orange?"

"What which-is orange?" Tim asks her.

"Tim give apple which-is green," Lana says.

Tim tells her, "No apple which-is green."

Only then does Lana say, "Tim give apple which-is orange."

When Lana called the orange an "apple which-is orange," she was not naming it out of thin air. The answer was part of a back-and-forth exchange that included a couple of dead ends and a mistake.

Science calls for evidence that is thorough and that can be clearly interpreted. This is not always the case with animal language studies.

Primatologist Susan Savage-Rumbaugh has investigated apes' use of language with this set of symbols, called lexigrams, which represent words and ideas. Kanzi, a bonobo, communicates by pointing to the lexigrams.

When primates use ASL to answer questions, for example, it isn't always completely clear what they are signing. Trainers may have to interpret the apes' gestures. And it isn't always possible to be sure that the animals are not picking up unintended cues from their trainers, like Clever Hans.

People do two things with language: comprehend and produce. **Comprehending** is understanding what other people say. **Producing** is saying things that other people can understand. So far, animals seem better at comprehending than at producing. They also show a greater ability to answer our questions than to tell us things on their own. Most of animals' "statements" are one-word or two-word labels. Combinations like sentences, which use syntax as well as the names of things, are much rarer.

Scientists are still debating what to make of the studies in animal language. Most of them agree, though, that more research will be valuable. It may teach us more about how animals' minds work, and possibly about how human language evolved.

A young deer learns its way by following its mother, building a mental map of the locations and routes in its territory. The deer may use elements from several known routes to create a new route. This kind of cognition, or mental activity, is common in the animal world.

4. OTHER MINDS

The world of animal cognition is broader than biologists once thought. Recent studies, for example, have shown that fish recognize each other. They learn about the status of individual fish in a group by watching each others' behavior. They remember past encounters with other individuals, and they team up to work together on finding food and watching out for predators. These mental activities add up to the way fish think.

One approach to understanding how animals think is to study all the things they are good at, such as their ability to form "maps" of the world around them. Animals' cognition does not follow human patterns of thought and language, but it is perfect for their needs and environments.

Mental Maps

Many animals are good at finding their way home, or remembering complicated routes and territories. Scientists describe this as being able to form a kind of mental map. The map that guides a bird on its long migration flight probably does not look at all like a page from an atlas, however. The bird's map is not just a visual picture. It is made up of Earth's magnetic field, the position of the sun or stars, the shapes of landmarks, the colors of plants changing with the seasons, and memories of earlier flights.

Animals use things such as scents and landmarks to help them find their way. Sometimes they also use problem-solving skills, one form of cognition. An example of an animal using cognition to find its way would be a young deer that follows its mother from a pasture to a pond, and learns the route between the two. Later the deer discovers a route from the pond to a new hiding place in the forest. If the deer figures out how to go directly from the pasture to the hiding place by combining the two routes it already knows, it has created a new mental map.

Octopus Geography

Octopus researchers reported in 2007 that these brainy invertebrates were quick to learn geography. Octopuses and cuttlefish (another type of cephalopod) were placed in aquariums that had been turned into mazes. The exit from each aquarium was at the bottom and could only be reached by a route around barriers such as jugs, piles of pebbles, and clumps of algae.

Once a cephalopod had found the exit, it remembered how to get to it the next time. The most important part of the experiment, though, was that each animal was learning two different mazes, in two different aquariums, at the same time. Thirteen of twenty-seven animals

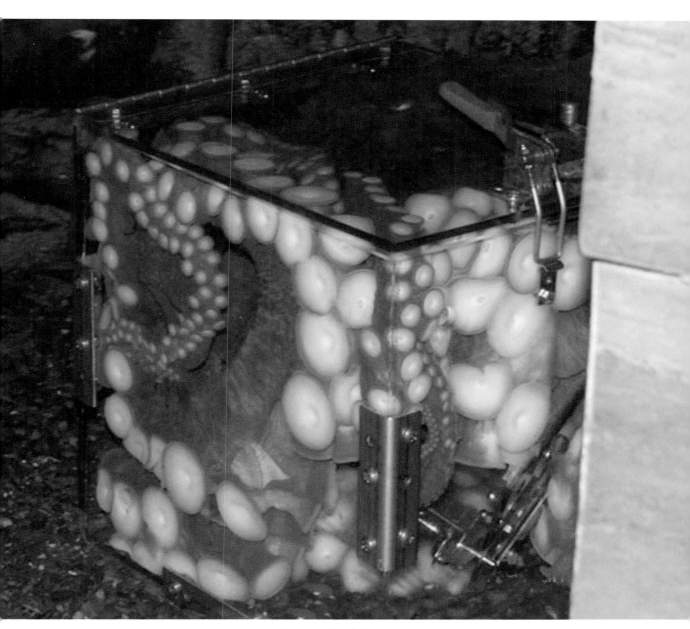

Truman, an octopus at Boston's New England Aquarium, surprised everyone by squeezing himself into a small box—then slithering back out. The box was part of a game in which Truman unlocked a series of boxes to get a food treat.

showed that they could switch from one mental map to another by successfully solving both mazes. When the scientists moved an octopus from one aquarium to the other, the animal switched from using the first mental map to using the second to find its way to the exit.

The cephalopods had shown a kind of thinking that scientists call conditional discrimination, which means using the correct behavior in different conditions. It was the first time that scientists had identified that kind of cognition in animals without backbones.

Time-Traveling Rodents

While one group of researchers put octopuses into mazes, a different team of scientists was discovering that meadow voles create mental maps involving both space and time.

Meadow voles are small rodents similar to mice. A male meadow vole's territory usually includes about seven adult females. He tries to mate with each of them as often as possible. From the male's point of view, the best time to approach a female is a few hours after she has given birth to a litter of young. At that time she is ready to mate almost immediately. A day or so later, however, she will be much less welcoming.

The researchers created a "vole dorm" for a group of female voles. Each female had her own compartment in the dorm. Some of the females had just given birth, some were almost ready to give birth, and some were very far from giving birth. After the females were set up in the dorm, male voles were allowed to explore the dorm for a short period of time. The rooms that were most interesting to the

Meadow voles are small mouselike rodents that seem to have a basic sense of time. In one experiment, male voles allowed for the passage of time when planning future actions, leading a researcher to call them "time travelers."

male voles were the ones occupied by females that had just given birth to their young. Then the researchers moved all the voles out and cleaned the dorm to remove the animals' scents.

Twenty-four hours later the researchers put the male voles back in the empty dorm. If the voles thought that nothing had changed, they would have gone to the rooms that had housed females that had just given birth. Instead, nearly all of the males went straight to the compartments where females that were close to giving birth had been housed the day before. The males had not only remembered which females had been in which rooms, but they had allowed for the passage of twenty-four hours from one day to the next. They ignored the rooms where females would have been ready to mate on the day before. They zeroed in on the rooms where they expected to find females that had given birth during the past twenty-four hours and would now be ready to mate with them. One scientist said the experiment showed that voles are "time travelers"—that is, they have a sense of time and do not live just in the present moment.

So . . . How *Do* Animals Think?

The simple answer to the question "How do animals think?" is "Not like people."

Most people are thrilled to discover that other animals in our world share some of our human qualities, such as the ability to add numbers or to make tools. As scientists find more and more evidence of animal cognition, barriers between humans and the rest of life continue to fall.

There will always be some barriers, however. Not just between humans and other animals, but between animals of different species. Each species evolved over millions of years to fit its own habitat and way of life. Each species is exactly as intelligent as it has to be, with its own kind of intelligence. Even animals that learn to use some of our words do not use them the same way we do. If an animal could learn 20,000 words, it would have a bigger vocabulary than most people—but would it ever tell a joke or write a story?

One mystery of animal cognition is that some individuals seem much more interested in learning things, or are "smarter," than others of the same species. Among humans there is a lot of variation in mental abilities. Scientists do not yet know whether animals have the same degree of variation, or less, or more. Remarkable animals, such as Rio the sea lion, Alex the parrot, and Koko the gorilla, may be rare geniuses in their species. Or will we find that their level of achievement is not so rare once we have studied more animals?

Research into animal cognition is still in the early stages. Many questions wait to be answered, but scientists have come a long way since the days of Clever Hans. There is now plenty of evidence that animals' mental lives are active and complex, even if we are never able to understand them completely.

GLOSSARY

anthropomorphizing	Thinking that animals' features, characteristics, and reactions are like those of humans; interpreting animals in human terms.
biology	Scientific study of living things.
cephalopod	Member of a group of ocean-dwelling invertebrates that includes octopuses, squids, and cuttlefish.
cognition	The act of thinking; mental activity.
comprehending	Understanding what others are saying.
conditioning	What happens when an animal or person learns that two things are linked, or associated.
equivalence	Recognizing that two things that are related to a third thing are also related to each other.
ethology	Scientific study of animal behavior.
evolution	Process by which new species develop over time because of changes, or mutations, in existing species.
instinct	Pattern of behavior that is genetically programmed, and that all members of a species are born with.

intelligence	Ability to learn, reason, apply knowledge, and interact with others and with the world.
invertebrate	Animal without a backbone.
object permanence	The ability to know that objects still exist even when they can't be seen.
predator	Animal that preys on, or hunts and eats, other animals.
prey	Animal that is hunted or killed by a predator.
primate	Group of animals that includes monkeys, apes, and humans.
primatologist	Scientist who studies primates.
producing	In language studies, saying things that others can understand.
psychology	Study of the mind.
social cueing	Giving signals—sometimes without knowing it—to other animals or people.
sociobiologist	A person who studies how animals that live in social groups interact with each other.
species	Group of plants or animals that are enough like one another to have offspring that are able to produce offspring of their own.
syntax	System of combining words in a certain order to create meaning.
zoology	Branch of biology that studies animals, including insects.

FIND OUT MORE

Books

Boysen, Sally. *The Smartest Animals on the Planet.* Buffalo, NY: Firefly, 2009.

Christie, Peter. *Well-Schooled Fish and Feathered Bandits: The Wondrous Ways Animals Learn from Animals.* Toronto: Annick, 2006.

Facklam, Margery. *What Does the Crow Know? The Mysteries of Animal Intelligence.* San Francisco: Sierra Club Books for Young Children, 2006.

Nichols, Catherine. *Animal Masterminds.* New York: Children's Press, 2004.

Page, George. *Inside the Animal Mind: A Groundbreaking Exploration of Animal Intelligence.* New York: Broadway, 2001.

Ryan, Marla Felkins. *The Planet's Most Extreme Thinkers.* Farmington Hills, MI: Blackbirch, 2004.

Steiger, Sherry Hansen, and Brad Steiger. *The Mysteries of Animal Intelligence: True Stories of Animals with Amazing Abilities.* New York: Tor, 2007.

Websites

Animal Minds
http://ngm.nationalgeographic.com/geopedia/Animal_Minds
This *National Geographic* site offers brief articles about animal intelligence, with links to and lists of additional resources.

How Smart Are Animals?
http://pbs.org/wgbh/nova/nature/how-smart-are-animals.html
This companion site to a 2011 episode of the science show *Nova* explores the intelligence of dogs, dolphins, octopuses, and Alex the parrot.

Inside the Animal Mind
www.pbs.org/wnet/nature/episodes/inside-the-animal-mind/introduction/2081/
This site introduces the three-part PBS series *Inside the Animal Mind*, originally broadcast on the PBS show *Nature*.

Mind & Brain/Animal Intelligence
http://discovermagazine.com/topics/mind-brain/animal-intelligence
Discover's Animal Intelligence page has links to dozens of articles about recent discoveries, written for everyday readers, not scientific experts.

Science Blogs: 5 Amazing Feats of Animal Intelligence
http://scienceblogs.com/neurophilosophy/2008/06/5_amzing_feats_of_animal_
intelligence.php
A brain scientist's blog that features video of animals such as crows and
elephants as they do things that indicate a higher-than-expected level of thought.

The Intelligence of Animals
www.cbsnews.com/stories/2008/10/19/sunday/main4531094.shtml
This brief, easy-to-read web page sums up a 2008 *CBS News* broadcast about
animal intelligence.

BIBLIOGRAPHY

The author found these books and articles especially helpful.

Adler, Tina. "Keeping Up with the Voles." *National Wildlife* (January 2010): 12–13.

Brown, Culum, Kevin Laland, and Jens Krause. *Fish Cognition and Behavior.* Ames,
IA: Wiley-Blackwell, 2006.

Burkhardt, Richard W., Jr. *Patterns of Behavior: Konrad Lorenz, Niko Tinbergen,
and the Founding of Ethology.* Chicago: University of Chicago Press, 2005.

Clotfelter, Ethan D., and Karen L. Hollis. "Cognition in Domestic Dogs: Object
Permanence and Social Cueing." *American Biology Teacher* 5 (May 2008): 293–298.

Coghlan, Andy. "Whales Boast the Brain Cells That 'Make Us Human.'" *New Scientist*,
November 27, 2006, www.newscientist.com/article/dn10661-whales-boast-the-
brain-cells-that-make-us-human.html (accessed 3/17/2011).

Cohen, Jon. "Thinking Like a Chimpanzee." *Smithsonian* (September 2010): 51–57.

de Waal, Frans. *The Ape and the Sushi Master: Cultural Reflections of a Primatologist.*
New York: Basic Books, 2001.

Fetzer, James H. *The Evolution of Intelligence: Are Humans the Only Animals with
Minds?* Peru, IL: Carus, 2005.

Gerardy, Justine. "Cape Town on Alert for Baboon-Jackers." *Mail & Guardian*,
May 4, 2010, www.mg.co.za/article/2010-05-04-cape-town-on-alert-for-baboonjackers
(accessed 3/17/2011).

Gould, James, and Carol Grant Gould. *Animal Architects: Building and the Evolution
of Intelligence.* New York: Basic Books, 2007.

Griffin, Donald R. *Animal Minds: From Cognition to Consciousness.* 2nd edition. Chicago: University of Chicago Press, 2001.

Griggs, Jessica. "Border Collie Takes Record for Biggest Vocabulary." *New Scientist* 2792 (December 25, 2010–January 1, 2011): 8.

Hatkoff, Amy. *The Inner World of Farm Animals.* New York: Stewart, Tabori & Chang, 2009.

Healy, Susan D., and Candy Rowe. "A Critique of Comparative Studies of Brain Size." *Proceedings of the Royal Society: Biological Sciences* 1609 (February 22, 2007): 453–464, www.ncbi.nlm.nih.gov/pmc/articles/PMC1766390/ (accessed 3/17/2011).

Krützen, Michael, and others. "Cultural Transmission of Tool Use in Bottlenose Dolphins." *Proceedings of the National Academy of Sciences* 25 (June 21, 2005): 8939–8943, www.pnas.org/content/102/25/8939 (accessed 3/17/2011).

Laing, Aislinn. "Baboons Learn to Listen for Cars Central Locking Tweet before Breaking In." *Telegraph*, July 23, 2010, www.telegraph.co.uk/news/worldnews/africaandindianocean/southafrica/7904436/Baboons-learn-to-listen-for-cars-central-locking-tweet-before-breaking-in.html (accessed 3/17/2011).

Linden, Eugene. *The Octopus and the Orangutan.* New York: Dutton, 2002.

Manning, Aubrey, and Marian Stamp Dawkins. *Animal Behavior.* Fifth ed. Cambridge, UK: Cambridge University Press, 1998.

McCarthy, Susan. *Becoming a Tiger: How Baby Animals Learn to Live in the Wild.* New York: HarperCollins, 2004.

O'Connell, Caitlin. *The Elephant's Secret Sense: The Hidden Life of the Wild Herds of Africa.* Chicago: University of Chicago Press, 2007.

Pepperberg, Irene. *Alex and Me.* New York: HarperCollins, 2008.

Talbot, Margaret. "Birdbrain." *New Yorker*, May 12, 2008, www.newyorker.com/reporting/2008/05/12/080512fa_fact_talbot?currentPage=all (accessed 3/17/2011).

Uhlenbroek, Charlotte, ed. *Animal Life.* New York: Dorling Kindersley, 2008.

Wasserman, Edward A., and Thomas R. Zentall, eds. *Comparative Cognition: Experimental Explorations of Animal Intelligence.* New York: Oxford University Press, 2009.

Wynne, Clive. *Do Animals Think?* Princeton, NJ: Princeton University Press, 2004.

———. *Animal Cognition: The Mental Lives of Animals.* New York: Palgrave, 2001.

INDEX

REBECCA STEFOFF has written many books about animals for young readers of all ages. Her book *Ant* was made into a chapter in a popular reading textbook for second graders. Since then Stefoff has written ten books, including *Horses*, *Penguins*, *Chimpanzees*, and *Tigers*, in the AnimalWays series for young adults. For the same publisher's Family Trees series, she explored twelve groups of living things, from *The Fungus Kingdom* to *The Primate Order*. Stefoff lives in Portland, Oregon, where she enjoys bird-watching, kayaking, and visiting the zoo. You can learn more about her and her books for young people at www.rebeccastefoff.com.